I0753237

Sports

for kids age 1-3

by Dayna Martin

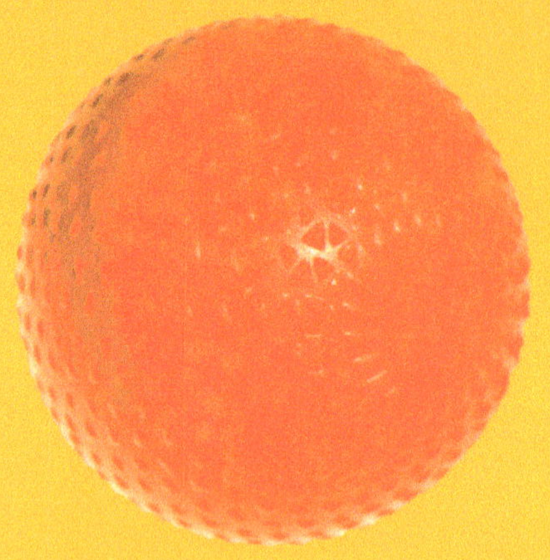

ENGAGE BOOKS

Mailing address
PO BOX 4608
Main Station Terminal
349 West Georgia Street
Vancouver, BC
Canada, V6B 4A1

www.engagebooks.ca

Written & compiled by: Dayna Martin
Edited & designed by: A.R. Roumanis
Photos supplied by: Shutterstock & iStock

FIRST EDITION / FIRST PRINTING

LIBRARY AND ARCHIVES CANADA CATALOGUING IN PUBLICATION

Martin, Dayna, 1983–, author
Sports for kids age 1-3 / written by Dayna Martin ; edited by A.R. Roumanis.

(Engage early readers : children's learning books)
Issued in print and electronic formats.
ISBN 978-1-77226-095-3 (paperback). –
ISBN 978-1-77226-096-0 (bound). –
ISBN 978-1-77226-097-7 (pdf). –
ISBN 978-1-77226-098-4 (epub). –
ISBN 978-1-77226-099-1 (kindle)

1. Sports--Juvenile literature.
I. Roumanis, A. R., editor
II. Title.

GV705.4.M37 2015 J796 C2015-903418-3
C2015-903419-1

Sports

for Kids age 1-3

Engage Early Readers

Children's Learning Books

by Dayna Martin

ENGAGE BOOKS / VANCOUVER

Baseball

Basketball

Soccer

Volleyball

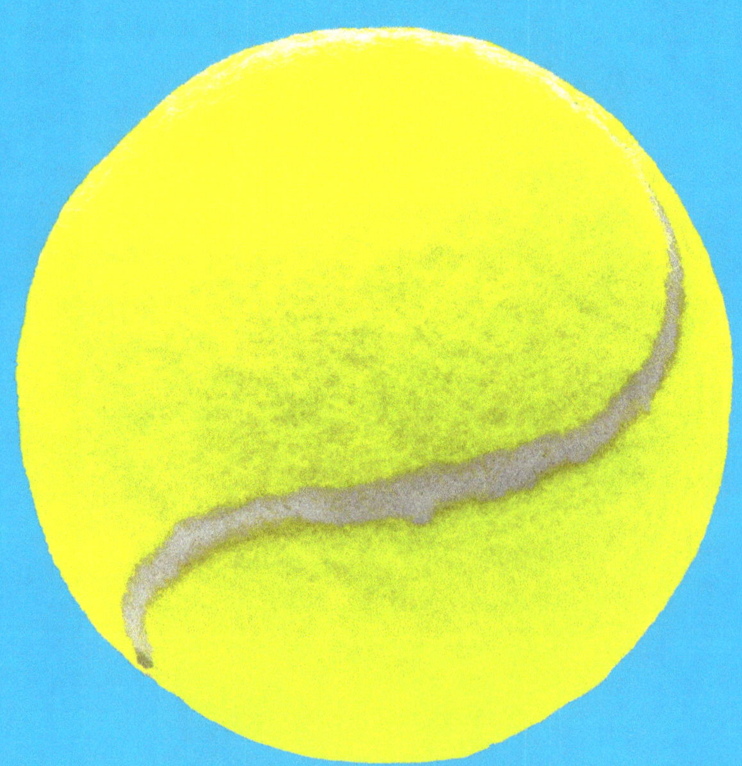

Tennis

CHAMPIONSHIPS

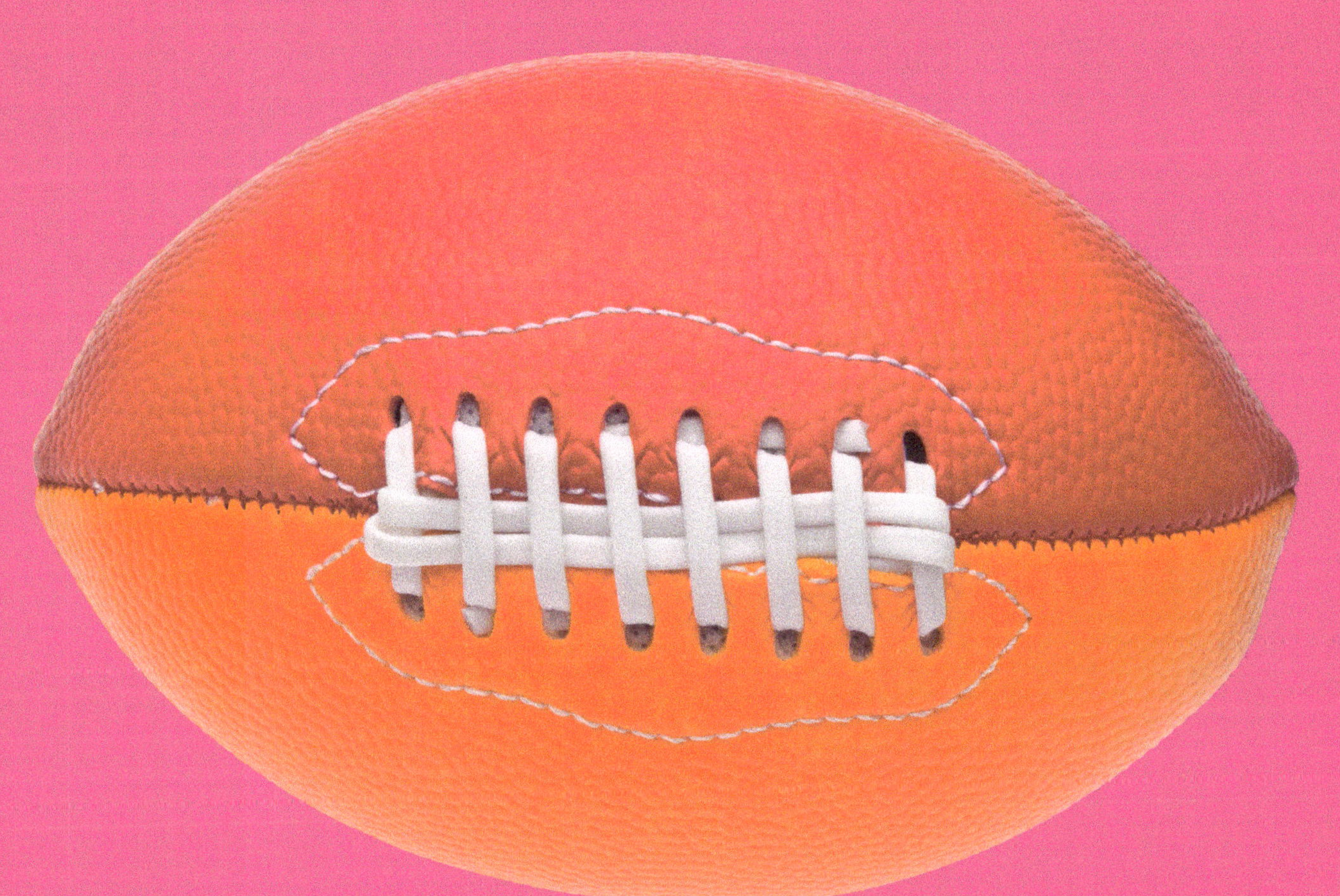

Football

Golf

Hockey

Softball

Badminton

Lacross

Water polo

Billiards

Ping pong

Cricket

Field hockey

Do you know what these sports are called? Can you find **basketball, golf, football, soccer, baseball, hockey, badminton, tennis,** and **volleyball**? Match the names to the pictures below.

Answer: football

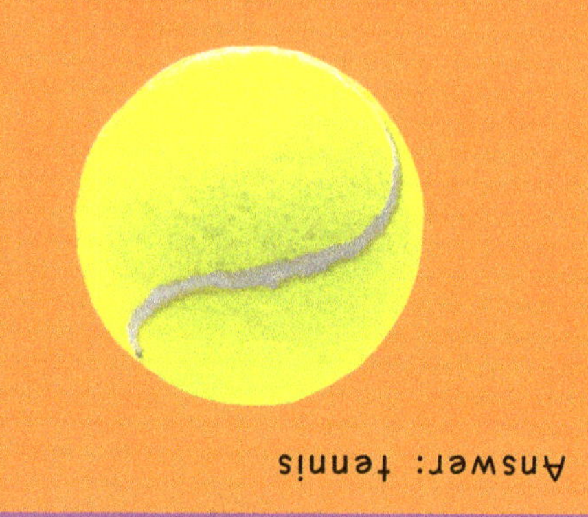

Answer: tennis

Answer: hockey

Answer: baseball

Answer: basketball

Answer: soccer

Answer: golf

Answer: badminton

Answer: volleyball

For other books in this series visit www.engagebooks.ca

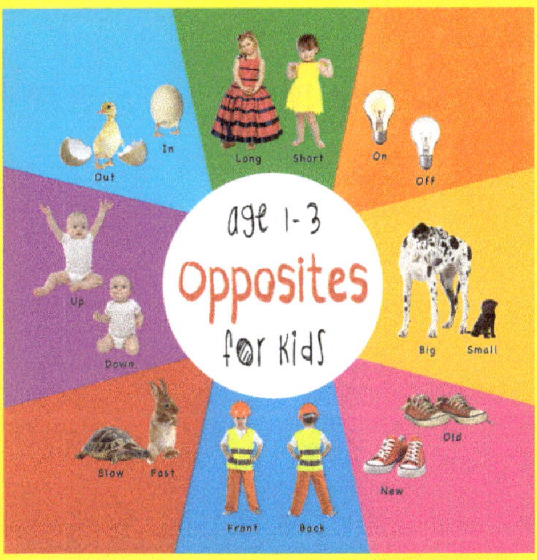

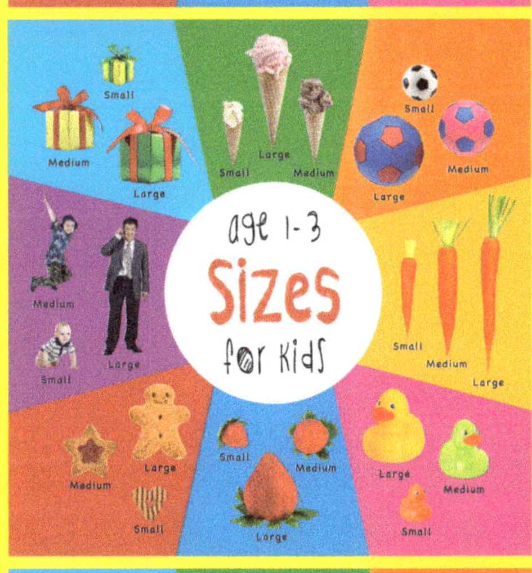

www.ingramcontent.com/pod-product-compliance
Lightning Source LLC
LaVergne TN
LVHW070918120826
845154LV00019BB/24
9781772260960